THE VOLATILE PRINCIPLE

BY

STEFANIE BENNETT

ISBN: 978-93-89690-82-8

First Edition: 2020
Rs. 200/-

Cyberwit.net
HIG 45 Kaushambi Kunj, Kalindipuram
Allahabad - 211011 (U.P.) India
http://www.cyberwit.net
Tel: +(91) 9415091004 +(91) (532) 2552257
E-mail: info@cyberwit.net

Printed at Repro India Limited.

ACKNOWLEDGEMENTS

Some of the poems in this collection have been published
by Southerly Magazine, Virgo Gray Press, Beyond The
Rainbow, The Lake Journal, The Paterson Literary Review,
The Foundation Of Australian Literary Studies, Message In
A bottle, Project Agent Orange, UFO Gigolo, The Bijou
Review, Indiana Voice Journal, Boston Poetry Magazine,
Cave Press, Mad Swirl, Dissident Voice Magazine, Eskimo
Pie, VerseWrights, Haggard and Halloo, Orbit Net, Every
Writer's Resource Magazine, Open Mouse Poetry, Shadow
Craft, Kind Of A Hurricane Press, Poetic Pacific, Wild &
Woolley, Dead Snakes, Illuminations Galaerie, The Poetry
Zine LA, Poetic Diversity, Rasputin, The Echo, The Scarlet
Leaf Review, Muse Magazine, The Galway Review, Famous
Reporter, Walleah Press, Poetry Super Highway... others.

CONTENTS

TIME-LINE QUOTES

With certainty the poems ring truer than most shining in the poetic filaments of this country. (Dimitris Tsaloumas)

One of the most original voices speaks through the great spirits of poetry and they through her. (Judith Rodriguez)

The subject matter of the poems range widely. Stefanie Bennett is a skilled word-smith. (Michael Dugan)

If peace is in need of an advocate then Bennett is a good one. May the hem of her skirts be stitched with hundreds of doves of raw silk. (Keith Russell)

Thank goodness somebody thinks poems are forever... what you say of Tsvetayeva may as well apply to you.

(Judith Wright)

This book is dedicated to the Paugussett Indian Nation of Connecticut USA & the uniting of Arts Action for Peace, the ACF, the CFA along with many others who called for 'a nuclear free world' under the heading of ICAN – The International Campaign to Abolish Nuclear Weapons. I am proud & indebted to my lot for having won the 2017 Nobel Peace Prize.

Extract: 'Art in the Light of Conscience'

I don't love life as such; for me it begins
to signify to acquire weight & meaning
only when it's transformed, that is, when
it is art. If I were to be taken beyond the
ocean into Paradise, & forbidden to write
I would refuse the ocean & Paradise.......

[Marina Tsvetayeva]

THAW

A dam is opening its gates in your eyes – .

Perhaps
        the snow on your eyelashes has melted.
Perhaps
        you are visualising some lost country.
Perhaps
        a lone thought like a passing love twinges.
Perhaps
        our time has gone sour.

Perhaps that blackbird at the window-pane
signifies what I can't explain:

        a dam
        opening
        its gates

        your eyes...
        metaphysics.

THE PACIFIC LANDSCAPE

'Yet the word is true
    plucked by a path
        where human vision went.'

             (Judith Wright).

ROSA ALBA AND THE VOLATILE
PRINCIPLE: Text and Commentary

Look! The most brazen
of skies where an outlined
bylateral head
twists off
its thunder.
Prophetically
outraged it
encounters
the era of
Hades benefactors
adorned in mock
three dimensionalism.

Times transparently past
should have taught
of the spirited
Buckle legend...
the gateway;
the two circles
intersecting.
Now, the old order's
misfired – and
talismen
invert
our star-spread.

Note how a collage
of barbed crowns
howl through
a harbouring

daylight misdiagnosed
as plexiformed
geophysics:
heat-fluxed
Astrologers
foolishly
ascribe The Ides
Of March.

Amphibious vetoing
and power's
obsession
uproot
the lotus...
Sirius
dog days
stall before
the fall
of this
stellar beacon
while

Set darkness
has become
the lone
hieroglyph.
Indeed,
the moon's
a forlorn
mistress
ever
searing
out her
Red King's

stone calendar.
Thus
exorcized, she
enacts
Isis by way
of Alchemy's
mercurial trap-door
as the Earth
rotates
      dizzily
on the lost
emerald
wings of
the tantra
      … Taurus.

AFFILIATION

How to address the hollowness
that looks out
from an old friend's eyes?

Much is demanded of the observer,
far more than the one
salvaging the desire.

Affiliations are catching. Just
search your pockets. You'll find smoke
but there'll be no fire...

most of us are in this state
of rehabilitation constantly
meeting another's demise.

People of the earth, there is
a conspiracy to keep us
leaning away from ourselves.

Believe in the universal petition.
Learn to look into a cripple's eyes
and say... I know you.

PROSAIC IT IS

Someone is practicing free verse
outside the brawling pub.
The round-house has three
gables and an auction sign
riveted to the driveway's
fresco wall.

Walk a crooked metre. You could
be anywhere! In the half-dark
the river's sludge dissolves
and an early moon casts a halo
that deftly skims towards a barge
tethered to its land-line.

This is a proportioning of the Pacific's
shore. The derelict
camp and two
                suspecting
patrol-cars wailing
towards the quay.

Lights deflect the harbour, form a web
of pale beads. Ah! Prosaic it is...
enough to climb the canvas, dip the blunt
negative into a boot-black shining
to curl about the suggested
free verse, rolling

and 'any-man' shouting
Charles Dickens.

EXTENSIONS

All evening spent under
the blue glaze of her eyes
and the imported night-shade
of a once fine satin.

The hop-scotch designed socks
she knitted in her nation's colours...
only three pairs, that time
because of the talking.

'It's getting close to winter
over there', is what she said.
'Always, someone's at some front.'
Then... tiredly

'Always children. So cold. Threadbare.'

The needles were ridged. Twisted.
· But they sufficed. Loyally
they'd worked fifty taut years.
'Hands...' she said. 'My needles are hands

… you know? Extensions of the heart.'

She died, on an over-cast day.
In Balmain it was.   [*suburb, Sydney, Australia]
How many knew she lived?
Only the land-lady and those

who dig graves for paupers
… and I, and a Polish
postman whose load
had been lightened.

ARTISAN: NORTH ISLAND

The bone carver
works at
the heart
of the matter
… weds mortal
to its other-half
with tools
as lean
as acquired logic.

Some dream polisher;
the calm
dexterousness
of race-formed
memory
appendixed
aeons before
that hoarded
Tasman crossing.

Not for him
the near Gods,
Haka... or
reptilian myths:
just white cloud
strung between
osmotic gravity
that grows
within his fingertips.

A rare gift. Blood
on the tourist dollar.

THE CONTEMPORARY

This contemporary. This whatever
you want to call it.
This small capital 'i' prefers
things that don't have
a stamp of grandness upon them.

I'm an embosser, by habit.
Antiquated antique thoughts arouse
all that's grounded in me.
Someone once said 'There's too much
earth in your mouth.' I agree.

I choose to dig my way
beneath sunsets. Never
would I suggest the tide
change its course. The real
need not shout a reason to be.

So! There's mud on my boot-soles
and aquatic sap in my eye.
My birthmark is mammalin
and I'm moon-struck
        … not by cosmonauts
but winged common courtiers of sky.

Exotic inquisitors damn inheritances.
Cut the throats of flowers.
Speak the machine's monologue
and programme what's known
as an inspirational hour. So...

To play second-fiddle, I submit, is as fine
as the wood weathered
to time. I breathe through
its resonance my own
elemental sound... meanwhile...

This contemporary
                belongs to
                        no man:
                                no man.

DISCOURSE – Pascal Style

Just because the postman
careers by
empty handed.
The Linden tree
bears no fruit.
And friends travel
on a mistaken
devil-may-care tide
doesn't mean that
the inconspicuous one
'in waiting'
won't attend
the Chekov soiree's
defining principle

of
    the first singer:
of
    the last song.

'AND WE GIVE EACH OTHER OUR TRUTH,

OUR KNOWLEDGE. A TEXT BOOK CAN'T

TEACH THAT'

Burra Gutya (Ken Canning)

STILL LIFE WITH FOLDED WING

Risen to morning's orchestration:
the flame tremolo of lorikeet
and the siren of black cockatoo.

In my field-watcher's eye
the sunflower splash is
juxtaposed by desert rim and space.

Totemic rock-wallaby, still
as sphinx, studies time's needle.
Around her wild grasses wave.

Knuckle-bones lie in wait
amid the turquoise hue;
a spiriting mandate.

What nebulous prophecy cups
the dawn star down? Whose
shadow's cross-stitched the sun?

There is question and reply.
I hoist my swag
and think on this...

walk backwards into early light.

STATUES

Opaque eyes in the thicket,
what is it
you're staring at?

Tibrogargan tragedy. Murmur
and muse: Mar-poor-am's all
that's left of the tale.

Damned to speak - I say,
of the running spear.
The lubra who mothered the moon.

Or, how the nomadic light
was on the wane
and white thunder

kicked back mountain, gorge:
cocked the trigger...
laid chaste mia-mia remains.

I am silent now,
as you are silenced.
The volcanic sleep erases all.

Still, my blood seeps uphill;
gently. Gently.
Kin to this

sad country I calculate
the weeping
water-colours of the day.

DINGO LINEAGE

High-tech hermetic groans
from the parapet...
that's an inner city paraphrase.
As they say; living is diatomic.

Later, outbound where highway
meets the sun
head-on, a pencil line
of long division calls me home.

Ladybird clinging to the windshield
… you migrate with finesse;
colour strapped
in speed and earthen light.

Stopped outside a country hotel,
the last groundswell
before that spinifex
regime flows over

you alight with me – taking your place
on the veranda rail. You click out
the most yellow of songs
… something to do

with space molecular.

WILLOW DREAMING

Drought's my season. Red earth
the soliloquy. Even
this creek bed's cut its losses.

Moribund crab-apple, you recognise
my skull, your old playmate
gone dissonant with haze.

Churlishly, I once believed
I could douse fire up
and fan it back again

but I am no overlord; the odd
monsoon puts quiet to that.
Born victims, let's not forget

our origins. Too adroitly fate's
equated to obstinacy; deliverance
grounded on hearsay.

Still, the moon's stark full of mystery
and land's ageing evermore.
I salute us with dust... with passion.

Watch the miraging rivers run.

KABUKI

In the crook of the season
a lone dragonfly
hurtles head-first
into the man-made lake.

From the bank I watch
the suicide. How to
interpret an insect thought?
How echo it back?

This amphitheatre's foreboding enough.
Humans rush to
a stop-watching dynasty
with gyroscopes transplanted into hearts.

It won't do. Stretch! Strike out!
... Becoming the kamikaze
stream of consciousness
means so much

less of you – claims
the otherness
of others.
Is this what we're resurged for?

The sigh that rises
from the lily-pad
has a diabolical lilt
                    ... it's over.

I trudge benignly homeward, mourn
the large life; the small death of it all.

SYMPOSIUM

The moon drags like an old stylus.
Earth sounds cackle...
a drooped sparkler on the blink.

Dark guests afford my open door.
Blue stockinged Blake.
Kafka in worn slippers.

How many titles have tumbled down
from the shelves!
How many mirrors are left to sack!

At least I can forget about reflections
... am no longer
afraid in looking back.

I put the midnight sun out to cool
by winter's wood-pile:
call forth Phantasm's cat.

That's too tall an order.
It sits in the peach tree,
tail flicking

... a silver mouse-like poet
surreptitiously pocketed
within the teeth.

Such ghoulish consternation.
The reminder
how fashion's destined for us.

MAGI AND THE LOTUS [*Roland Robinson: Jindywrobaks]

All night long I've called the new moon down:
shuffled compliance plates -,
played strip-jack with the stars.
This metamorphosis of wizardry
is a stilling tide
that laps the gourd's compendium.

And I'm recounting Roland, wrapped
in a theorist blanket
of nocturne stringy-bark,
striding out
the mangrove reach
via the whip-bird's own short-falling.

Led now to the Minotaur's betrothal,
Old Woman Island silhouettes
a dancing salt-toned Gaia.
Dispassionately she threads
the 'seven sisters' about
her camp-fire oval.

Far off I hear the cadenza, booming!
Middle Earth's song sticks. 'Beautiful   *
my leave-taking...' follows the innuendo
of a meteorite soundless in its trawling.
"Del Espiritu Santo" pays hospice
to a back-dropping everness – and

the drift of things unfolds a banksia sky
... opalesque, if shrouded
                              within the script
                              of morning.

THE FORCE

Don Juan, in this quaternary age,
wears a tattered Akubra
and sings
the purple spoils of poetry.

Out there, where hawks cross-cut
picture postcards
and the still chattering
chimney stones are

reminiscent of a penal code
dead as death
to mindless bureaucracy,
our 'rake' squats

in the quasi-fallout of things.
He has done time
in 'Nam; elsewhere; has
swallows for eyes.

Contemplate. He'll be President
any day now.

(rake = dissipated man)

MARGINS

On my return to Windy Gap
all the birds of the air
sobbed red and deep;
and – the Volga roared
at the foot
of an ice-slabbed shed

I swear I saw a bitter harvest.

Forced labour! The tragic slogan
All FOR THE FRONT
swung on the skull
of a parched star.
A voice said - "Attempt
                    Translation."
Rolling out
the samizat swag,
I did.

ENCYCLOPEDIA OF SOUND

It was nothing. A dream is nothing.
I refuse to discuss it, we
dissect too much.

It was nothing. One war is nothing.
If it led to another
that's what wars are for.

It was nothing. A life is nothing.
We all have a touch of it,
a fine, a very slick fixative – no more.

It was nothing. Death is nothing.
Places are vacated, are
filled-in quicker than an open crypt.

Nothing is nothing until someone
signs its truth. Find it
between the ears,

the burned out eyes – the shovel
of earth wedged
in its mouth.

FAITHFULNESS for Olga Berggolts

Pressing my two palms together,
finger-tips lightly touching
I create an atlas -
a minor world
where citizens sleep
… sometimes fitfully.

House of death's asphalt,
how abstract
you've become
below the dome of sky
as thumb-balls
crack the glass

cheekbones
        in Kiev,
            in Canberra.

THE EXCHANGE

Au revoir! Now I borrow from myself
and watch my peerage
exorcise those pastoral roots.

Conversely – it is – must be, all one.
The scaling down of Yeats
to Devil's Rock

and across the experimental pastiche
of the senses into
the mirage of tomorrow

in a space where Eros dust serves
its theatre in-the-round
with canticles,

formed out of bracken, knowing
analogies for
the cosmic dance they are.

PROLOGUE for The Tsarskoselsky Muse
[USSR Writers' Peace Forum, 1987]

Such a conditional catch-cry
one trembles
to utter it. And where
once stood Petersburg
now stands
that watermark;
an antipodean centrefold.

Akhmatova... pious bell ringer!
Helix. Euphemistic tormentor.
A cartload of straw
bears its strange burden
throughout city square
            … and onto that
your name – a sea
of steepled hands burning.

Above sear the wings of Punin
become autumnal rags
to wrap your
iconoclasm in.
You lie sallow; vindicate
the metaphysical
kiss of nations.

Salutation's wry comfort across
an evensong's wailing wall.
Still, what else must I give
wild coloratura
but this? My own
prospecting Acmeism;
this belated neo-stanza.

FUTURES

I think we lived in a loft, then.
Times were solid, so too
the immune system
of the heart's terrain.

Toils of trial and error
leaked through our imagination.
Winds rocked the sparrow's nest
above the hatch-way.

Still, all hung together. I suspect
an innocence reigned
and gave cheer. We were
mutineers and didn't know it.

What double-edged siege or storm
sent us askew and wandering
is now past my recall:
you get on with the learned and leaving.

A modest retirement village
geographically covers
the place we once posed in.
                              New blood
cavorts about the wicker-chairs.

Perhaps all futures begin with
lofts and sparrows
and twilight rain... and a sure hand
on the tiller.

Sentiments aside, I choose to believe that.

TRIADS

From the Ta-ku-shi

(Itinerant singer and story-teller)

Opening quotes by

Dorothy Auchterlonie.

(1)

"One cannot condemn a tree because
 it has a few dead twigs."

A row of birches, splendidly adorned
in silver arrows
lead the way
to this village.

Po Chu-i... fading
near-bankrupt poet,
resides within
the old temple

and today's crisp calendar
bids him 'kneel'
before a Summer
stricken peach tree.

Blossom-less, coarse limbs
are lifted
in a last apostrophised
shout to heaven.

If Calvary shone in another
erstwhile place
neither knew
of that event...

but sure resolve elevated
the Sage
and formed
the internment

where man and wood make one.

(2)

"If a man were to give all the substance of
his house, it would be utterly contemned."

Four walls contain acquaintances:
Table and chairs,
immensely relevant.
As well – the wine cup.
The ticking clock, and
neatly folded paper money
to nurse me through
an oncoming second life.

Here, in plenitude, abides the astringent
light of Eastern Nigredo.   *
Perhaps the copper
fire-grate
will become an emerald
the size of
that September moon
upending treasure's residue.

Outside, each morning, a mottled dove
archaically laments
to a sky-full
of flowers.
I must ask
the ornithologist why
it appears
the voice is broken.

{* Alchemical cleansing of The Philosopher's Stone into black.}

(3)

"Why are the soldiers off to war?
Oh, grand sire, tell me please..."
They fight to right their wrongs,
My dear, and ward off enemies."

Everyone has a pseudonym:
ruptures in debenture – tundra
reckoning of the soul. It's
what's done with these. Whether
to surrender to the yoke?
Splay out upon the wheel.

The veritable fox at the water-trough
holds my gaze,
seems pacifistically personified
in surrounds of wild violets
and grasses
as green as memory.

In effigy, the road-signs of his eyes
tell of places
such as Xanadu. Slipping
into the blue
veiled mandala I can
accord or stall the fable.

A NOTE ON YANNIS RISTOS

Throughout the Axis occupation of Greece (1941-1945) Ristos was a member of the National Liberation Front and wrote poems for The Greek Resistance. He supported the left in the Civil War and in 1948 was arrested and spent four years in prison camps. Again, in 1967 he was sent back to prison in Gyaros, Samos and Lemos. His poetry was banned. The French poet, Louis Aragon, has said that Ristos was "The greatest poet of our age."

After Yannis Ritsos

Song-cycle

And when they ask me what I have seen
I shall say I remember nothing.

[Randolph Stow]

WITNESS

If, once in a show of ambiguity,
tubular chimes are
stashed about the attic;
a cat-o'-nine-tails
hangs twitching
from the eaves,
and dextrin rests
the door inoperative...

No conjuring is required
to define the man
waxing glacial bat wings
on the hearth.

Know only that he flew
the Aegean
surveillance
free – deposited
'Songs of the Motherland'
within
your crucible and left
the confessional
early.

DOWSING

One blade of grass
will weather all seasons,
trawl a spider's thread
through the chimera wound
as D-Day approaches.

Listen. Do you hear the crib
shrieking empty
in the holster
of the wind? That's
convergence!

One blade of grass...
                    flexible,
covets the key
to antiquity
and slays
the Discus Thrower.

Not of this era – passers-by mistake
transparency for rubble.

BENEDICTION

No. I won't talk to the angel. Not yet.
I'm responsible
for lifting the blindfold:
for the sun's cauterised dart — and
the fountain-pen's fury.

He kicked the steeple's projection
and sat
cross-legged
in the void he'd discerned
via a rainbow's coccyx.

Unperturbed, Orion's belt buckle
fell, chuckling
and cleansed
the sod
from his feet.

KISS

Dexterity was put on hold
as the bombs dropped.
Submissively, the woman
tossed coarse salt
over both shoulders,
steadied the cut-glass pitcher,
and folded curd
in a spotted napkin.

When the panting corridor of air
spiralled
it slapped
the courtyard child,
her child
          oblivion-bound.
Omitted is the sound
of love's collision.

RESISTANCE

In the basement the scent of cloves
rivalled rising tear-damp
along a torn curtain.
'Subversion,' he said, 'must be
the down payment of war'
and fingered the stone crucifix
above the lice-plagued mattress.

Later, famine bruised the soil and
an embryonic Junta
came calling.
A pencil stub
            was found
deftly piercing
the vast
interior sky.

ERRAND: For a Lost Sister

Weariness died, and in the hollow
of your eyes
again I gather
white migrating birds
textiled against
the midnight sun.

Tomorrow, I pledge – I'll cameo
a locket of
hyacinth-blue dolphins
washed with silver...

You'll see!

Watch them frolic
the avenging straits
away
... deity adorned.

PROOF

Quickly; Pablo! Invert the canvas. Upon us
attests 'The Book Of The Dead.' *
Add crocus yellow
spiked with garnet
to line her eyelash
before the flash of life fades.
Rouge – I tell you, won't soften
the cheek. Instead
fashion the brow's panorama
and dimple a linden leaf
that pipes melodic.

Master of the cuneiform palette,
let's forfeit
the signature corner.
"Guernica"
and our Philadelphia vixen
are companionable.

* Muriel Rukeyser

COIL

Because the asphodels reminded him
of his mother he placed them
in a jar on the balcony
where the owls wept at eventide.
Leaving... the gate
unhinged itself,
pirouetting the balustrade
to shower the shutters
rust-shut.

What was left
stayed inevitably the same

except for
the dissident
moon-raking mercenary
wearing
a black armband
and hand-me-down
combat boots.

FREEZE

It's official. Some of us were scapegoats
balancing on the tip
of tyranny's thumb
seeking incandescent statutes
by way of compromise.

Still others... the blessed
ordinary, come to mind.

The ones cushioning a prisoner's
ribcage after the bird
had flown.
The sandal-maker
detonating chains, and
the ventriloquist
vocalising 'Romiosini' *
under an informer's gaze.

These – the jaws of the earth #
will claim.

(poem by Ritsos – 'Greekness' *)
[appears on a fresco in Cyprus #]

SANTORINI SOLO

How cruel. How inept. The harpoon
grounding the beach-head!
Waves cut and run – but
the starfish agitates
a shallows' silt
discarding pieces of eight.

What was it the Archer illusioned?
The sirenian
combing her sea-green hair.
The pumice collector, wrinkle grey
or the last shield-bearer's
unsheathed sword.

The pebbles – keepers of faith,
openly bled
        rallying
the mainsail's
dismissal;
the collapse of decks.

TORQUE

Fifteen steps to the mortuary *
and the taste of lime
on his tongue.
He walks slowly. Attention
would bring him undone, put paid
to the collateral
snug in its jacket lining.

At the barricade
                    … a tip-off.
This time they
take him alive.
From the furnace of his chest
issues mesolithic moths
and soot – eternal.

*Fifteen is the traditional syllable line count
 for Greek folk songs.

THE RED ROAD

'The only part of us they cannot steal
is what we know'

(Wolf Who Waits)

OWING IT ALL

They talk of corn – Caribbean blue;
tri-gold; matt-white.
Geordie, Tipperary tigress
astride her sun-kissed vale.
Vittoria, immigrant: mother
to five at eighteen light years
and Melissa, stately in deer-hide
polishing a nation's bloodstone.

"You are the husk of a dawn-star."
They intone, 'You are
what's left of the coup.'

        I am the Straw Woman
        cross-stitching
        my own eyelids
        where
        the bone walk's
        one half octagon
        away.

CREST

I have aged by my crying river where the water-weed
harbours a sodden almanac.
In this hemisphere the rain
tendrils red upon
a parched heart, its shape
abstruse – a dropped star.

Well recounted is the quest of 'the other'. Pacing
out Endurance Road. Wolf Song Woman
wrote her dust epigraphs
on the boots of fishermen;
the silver-forks of 'dame fortune'
and – the high-fliers in repose.

From Quebec to Armenia. Bombay. Sydney town...
she unravelled the dialects;
strung them out
to be mystically
arpeggioed by
diverse adepts of the mouth-bow.

And how rich was the sowing of the spirit fruit!
Each yield a hoop
of plenty. Both
huntress and gatherer, net offerings
graced the gilded halls
of 'poeticised' pogrom.

How many climbed aboard that bronze saddle?
        (she will not say).
What loss flash-flooded
the verdant oasis?
        (self-destruct? Premonition?

To this day the Seven
Living Sins
continue their vigil...

Indigo is the tranquil sleep-walker harnessed to
the crying river.
Vermilion the sickle moon.
Ash – the oration in any tone.
The fable?
Colourless. Pigment it gone.

LIBERTY

She lives on the fault-line
South-East of
the City of Angles
and could
            even as I speak,
out-snooker any rival.

At ninety-three, come fall,
she'll tell
how leaving the future behind
is a vocation,
            like Blackjack,
with the chips
duly scattered.

However, the soothsayer
            admits
there's one regret.

Passing-white was
an
    occupational
            hazard.

NEXUS

Santa Rosa was the favoured haunt
in early fall.
My aunt, grey eyes

flashing like moon-arrows
sought out
humming bird and quail,

her dilapidated camera
balancing on
bedrock mortar.

The snapshots were a breath
of yesteryear
unchanged;

past-holding postscripts
Coachella bound
and pending.

Later – we drank
the water-flask dry.
A toast

to Twin-horned Toro's spires.
The way it's done.
Operable. Received...

CRUSH

You have to step out of it,
the pain of being too concerned
with who devastated reason
and the cause
of why nightingales elude.

You have to

shake off the fear,
the by-products
on how later will count
glowing its true colours.

You have to

commence worshipping,
if worship you must,
names shot down while
practising an ideal.

You have to

recognise that monuments are
mountains and storm-drains
and loves that got away
recurring, again, as the wild card
in the hand of
                    show poker.

UNDISTORTED EXPERIENCE

It's growing up diagonally
at 64 and remembering
September 11
(not specifically because
cousin Ricki
was there...).

It's the tick-tacking accuracy
of whether anthrax spores
are absorbed
in our
hung-over
morning coffee...

Pseudo market forces,
PC hackers
          (Con amore)
or trilingual brokers
ensnared by
a crust of
bullion rising

that collars the phrase
we – become
what we deplete.

TRUMPS

More often than not she wore
slacks, plaid
patterned
and wide at the cuff.
Old golfers,
nine decades
down the divide,
are a lively breed.

I knew little but learned
some tactics
about stance, swing and
the 'hole in one'
captured during
'The Women's Open'
on Honolulu's green.
                    Annually
those trophies got dusted.

I reckoned time's expediency
wouldn't catch her
napping.
She'd knock back
a whisky, neat
and allow
the Charleston another
joint-creaking whirl.

It happened as I'd foreseen.

THE FIX

Mon dieu! I did not expect to find you splayed out
on the recliner
exuberant but bewailing

the new Great Recession's turn
around, land cheats – and
government laxity

that would make a penny squeal
louder than
bagged bobcats in midwinter.

'Go easy' was the best I could do.
'Don't forget
lumbago flares when...'

You sprang upright: stormed
to the baby grand.
Bach's "Sleepers Awake"

set the dog yowling off-key.
Apparition you were... how
I miss your state of grace.

HUSH

She died, and the micaceous almost summer winds
dizzily scudded across Arazona
via the Pacific Crest
piercing Sacramento's side.
Neither dust
nor blind intervention
rattled that topaz blue.

She left, with a casket of leaves embellishing
the motorcade, her wish
homely attuned
as it lassoed the sweet aroma
of ponderosa
and a spotted owl's
digital refrain.

This, the forest's logbook accentuates
in incised resin
the colour of rain – while Days of Our Lives
winged on cable,
and CNN's
disfigurement
abetted
the able.

CREATION'S CHANT for Judith Rodriguez

Do not wake me from
this dream. Do not
stir the pyre
or disturb one stone.
The wild-flowers are
in abundance
and the hills serene
with their own dreaming.

Whether it be noon
or night's haven,
the opposites console
and walk
a skyway fit for
the evolution of mammalia
and winged chariots
of soft gold.

To my right,
the marshlands murmur
legendary
music of
birch flute and drumming.
To my left, a desert
as bountiful and clear
as permanent spring.

In the distance
wise spirits ritualise
the song and dance
of the everlasting.
Behind me
a fearless rainbow
bends to kiss
the sacred ground.

Do not wake me
from this dream.
Do not tamper
with what quietude
remains in which
we live and die.
Do not wake me yet:
I'm not ready
            to face
my too human
murder.

TRYST

The log-house is like most others – elongated
and meant for rustic living.

Waup, whose ancestors stretch generations
busily skillets flat corn-bread

half mixed with maple syrup and mustard ginger;
the rest will accompany jalapeno dip.

Beneath the stern-eyed tin-plated portraits
newspapers sub-titled 'Noble Savages',

habitual Clan Mothers gather and discuss
a country's war profiteering.

The day rolls over into antiquity. Vigorously,
survival reinvents itself.

(Waup Athoo Kwey = White Fawn)

DESIGN

When he whispers incantations
across the ceremonial pit
in late winter
the last snow-drift
orbits the tree tops
like smoke
on a morning stroll
headed towards
infinity's skylight.

Praise abounds. The sun soars.
Raven gives a jocular
caw matched by
the smiling Elder
          who has
my father's eyes
          and more.

With hands wide open
we spread the wealth.

RELIC

Picking up shells on Long Island
I'm remembering a displaced people

as the thin sea's edge draws the firmament
in streaks of pale violet.

Trade-goods would have been exchanged here
… copper kettles for wild game,

squash – and field-fruits awaiting
the scorched Metacom's advance. *

I dig my heels into quick-silver sand
wet with the tide's ebb

and reel at a faint earth pulse.
All around are distinctive

indentations: moccasin shaped.

*Metacom = King Phillip

IMPETUOUS COUSIN for Kenneth

Naturally his leaving grieves me.
The .38 caliber colt
still pinioned
to the left-hand
trigger finger
                on the outskirts
of Connecticut's
heartland
is a sombre warning.

Never preach
tribal sovereignty
in the first instance,
in – the past tense.

TOTEMS

The Hereditary Chief – an ordinary man,
knows no reason to sing
his own swan song
in the beige frost
of dawn's solace.

Instead, a fax machine whirrs
direct officiates as
ethno-historical studies
glean consolidation from
                 the Netherlands,
to Leningrad, to Paris...

Objectively – he turns his back
on the technological plateau
and shuffles out
to greet the small world,

Gustoweha crowned –

headed towards the wolf
making his rounds.

ALONG THE LATTER-DAY

The most powerful presence is absence

(Dorothy Porter)

WIND SONG

> 'The life of a poem does
> not begin on paper.'
> (Y. Yevtushenko)

Forget me. Place me upon
your unwanted list.
Tell your friends –
tell your family,
this stranger was
no more than fiction.
Forget me. My words set
your head aching.
Your body,
a testimony
of too much ruin.
Your young heart
fit only for breaking.

Go now! Speak with authority
and confidence
on how to escape
the twin-selves; take
love's grey ashes
and bury them deep.
Laugh again... even
if the laughter's shallow.
Buy back
your spirit.
It will be cold.
Put on
a warm front.

This is what you wanted? Your ghost
has slipped within
the key-boards
of memory...
There's just an odd chord
you'll hear occasionally:
ignore it!
Forget me. Forget yourself.
The shutters
go on creaking. The new
moon's ablaze.
The night lawn
is silver – inside the room

the lamp
          is raining.

CLOSED EYELIDS, CLOSED WINGS

I prefer to talk to the dead:
the living have
given up their listening.
Those gone before
share my whisperings.
Quirks illusion.
Tears brined
on hot stone.

And when I step out
ex-officio,
I am never
segregated; alone.
I carry the bold genesis
of the Bronze Age: Iliad
threads caught in a coat
of Homeric undertones...

"Wherever I travel, Greece
wounds me." That enamel
cry – Serefis . I know
the Aegean once flowered
with corpses and
your Centaur's plight met
rabid dogs. Perhaps it turned
sailors into poets. But mute

rests the exotic post-exorcism
my reformer of Odyssey.
This; a wayfaring visitor

gathers the proclamations
your saddened
harvest held
within the breast
of the night's sun.

Ever dark; the cold
glistening chains!
Ever dark epistles defying
still darker ransom – the erosion
of power and hands
nailed blue-black
to the gunwale. Now
the tongue's attack...

"We are dying! Our Gods
are dying..." Not so.
One crippled monk
tends the door-key
to St Mama's.
Starfish scuttle
a pilgrimage
from Corfu, to Crete

to the new Renaissance
weight-bridge
… Athens...while
nearby a saffron
rose makes
peace with
the half moon.
Pine and juniper

are upstanding. I raise
the small
terracotta statue
to the heavens' might.
Aphrodite's lips
bloom
          scripted
                    continuance.

WEN AND THE RED CANDLE:
(Wen I-to executed in 1946)

Putting on my flag-ship colours...
my work boots. My worn gloves.
I go out to greet you, dark visitor.

You went by the way of the Western-bank.
You will rise, in that same place; this time
carrying the whole of China with you.

Brother poet, the chronicles have been
reshuffled. Thankfully
your works are no longer set alight.

No! I do not wish to cause discomfort, but
the news I bring is... desolate.
Millions now join you in exile.

Confidentially, there are no safe crossings.
Reason drifts with the river-wind.
We must turn again from the Tie-an-men.

All is circumspect, my dark visitor.
The garrisons of greed are treacherous and
conduct slavery quite openly. The Globe

of 'precious change' has shrunk
ten thousand times since
you blessed it with your tears...

As you prophesized, the 'dead water' has risen.
Peking's paper ghosts are the same
as their Western counterparts.

You said... 'build a bridge'...'cross over'!
Instead, they built a star-ship to heaven;
a red sun so bright
           none can see the way back.

I go out to greet you, dark visitor – your
old war-cry at my throat. Our white flag
is no surrender but a soiled heart
      tattered by grief.

AFTER 'THE UNDEFEATED' for J.R.

Time-slot? A sometime August. The book,
rather – the pamphlet – holds
the ingredients of another
Queenslander gone lame.
The Red Queen plaits her grief;
drops the assessments
into a brown river. The folds
of King George Square.
The university's hole-proof apron.

Much later we wheeled in 'The Cold.'
Again, a one-bar heater;
the place setting un-auspiciously quaint.
Poets and shanty towns
complement the over-occupied.
Cake – without frost. Coffee – non-sweet
at the double.
Didn't I say – the ear believes
what the heart forsakes?

Selected climatic graffito bursts from
that pre-loved folder.
I add a pinch
of salt. Contemplate... "I refuse
to let them die."
Meaning the versifiers
gone before
through the wintering
jaws of nonchalance.

You... envied... me! (tete-a-tete)
Choose a fate – any one.
Sweet-grass and sage
blends the smoked
bear-berry leaves.
These I import far below cost.
Ah... the one-bar hiccups,
near obsolete. Hand to mouth
living is snug; is contagious.

Outside, just for the record, we posed.
The wind-swept mountain
roared of guttural terrain
as cedar and oak
contorted – danced.
The storm bird quipped
and cloud covered. Recall,
I sent the black and white
copy and postcard?

Answers come and go. I read
of the 'red acquisitions'. Am privy
to what's called border-notes.
My smudging bowl
abundantly supplies opaque
signs of the endangered ones.
Yesterday – I swear I saw
old Mallku (Inca, for Condor)
... hovering.

MT. ETNA AND HORSES OF THE MOON
(A song for the azure cameo)

Now... finally, I want to carry the clear corn
resurrected in my grandmother's veil.
I want to place the selenium where
it must sustain the object
of this most cautious of customs to retain
forever the bread host's transmutation.

Smoke is rising from the chimney. I will,
bounteous mother, treat our guests
to a wake of your finery. Figs,
                              I have gathered;

tomatoes... and crushed almonds!
Sweet yellow wine is to be shared
with the herdsman's son and those
                                    from the grotto.
Not wastrel nor saint should
forget how you sang and nurtured here.

Concordantly, the eyelids will be covered
by the palms of your confettied hospice
as crickets hum in nearby thickets.
At Yuletide, I'll toss the sachet
of camomile into the lava's compendium

                              then lay down
                              with the corn,
                              with the veil.

MY MOTHER'S HAIR

My mother's hair was white
underneath the scheme
of things. Things grown out of
recognition – but that's the way it was.

The last time I saw her she'd taken
her new shoes out walking.
Fine shoes they were; Brazilian
leather. They willed themselves
                                back to me.

Most days she'd toil between sink
and table. All the while
whistling songs – those
evergreens the local radio
                                plays on demand.

Sometimes, there was a lapse into
silence. Eerie it was. As if
her thoughts had grown so loud the world,
her world, needed a protection only
                                she knew how to give.

The potted palm and herb garden
grew well to her
unending care. And I grew, as did
the summers, and the weeds
                                beside the creek.

Then the songs grew less – and toiling
slowed. She had taken to wandering
way past midnight. The white hair changed
to another hue: it matched the sheen of
                    Brazilian leather...

She'll not come back, though summer's here
bringing strange new weeds to the garden.
She'll not come back – I tell an opened door:
The white hair in the river-wind
                    knows the scheme
                    of things.

IRIS ORACLE After Rocco Scottalino

The dirty linen's tumbled after
that last cursed war:
my crest fallen uncle can't come back!

I've trecked from the shores of
San Remo, past cathedrals
that reek of Christian pitying,

to Valenza – where thirteen shrews
wail in their eventide black
                    beneath seven stars
forming the shape of the plough

… to find one stone commemorates you,
Giuseppe; partisan shot by Germans
and provisionals of Italian militia.

'And only my own kind will kill me'
wrote a brother
facing another diabolical accord.

Surely this is where grief spins
its curtain calling among
                         the fur trees:
the ritual of diametrical deceit.

Who's fallen? Never our national astronomer
or the ragged pennant
restored along with the invaders.

I taste the bitterness of sulphur
no scythe can cut clean;
Eci mettiamo a maledire insieme   (=) *

and "we begin to curse together."   (repeated) *
We – who've unbalanced
the blood-lore
                  still holding
                  Valhalla
                    proud.

*

Note: the italicised line is from
Osip Mandelstam

REMEMBERING Ken Slessor

And – did you stroll the rough-edged canvas
along Careela Street or
turn clockwise
north-east
at the canal?
On a cornflower blue day
distractions sear the paper-chase.
My neighbour tells... 'you wore
a greatcoat – were
variably discrete
but twirled
a cane.' Allows,
the joked strine-high
accent, 'saints alive!
Could have been a sideshow.'

And – did you tide-print new loaves, old fishes
down by
the wharf?
Make your way
to the local – sponge
a bitter pint of stout and
sing a mischief-round of
dervish rings... ritual observances?
The waitress confirms,
'Kept an eye
on the bay.
Asked if the Captain

[cuss him], waded ashore
to land-leg about
the coral coast of Capricornia.

And – come the thunder chant, sott'o vo'ce:
did the St. Elmo's fire flare green
beyond the head's
outcropped ledge enough
to circumvent
the predisposed
ox-blink and the incident?
That evening, flicker of cricket
and gaslight finds
indomitable cut-out minuets
risen from
the punch-holes of space.
Within the quarter-deck's
observatory a glass pentacle
           tolls a la mode. It is
the masked headless boy – who speaks.

TIPSTER

On nights of the full moon
I batten down
the hatch,
for who knows what city clickers,
layabouts and deceivers
will tally up to.

All and sundry is fumigated:
especially the wicker chair
belching collywobbles
and covered in hoar frost
… the lair where
an enthused meteor squats
and resumes his Promethean
shock-jock tale
of devil's dust
gone loco.

"Beware of pith and marrow,"
he intones.
"It's sucking eggs
that make
          wise counsel."

NOTES TO ANOTHER POET

It's the enigma of it all. And – as they
say in this country, I've a tendency
to 'bat the breeze'. Forsooth, I am
a talker but I also walk my tongue
into the heart of action.

Maybe... it's the blood spilled on
other shores. The pedigree
I refuse to mock. There, the hand
                    of campania valour
would tap me on the back... project,
'speech is richer when life's poor'.

So – I specify
                "a mouth was not meant
                to yawn
                itself to
                comfortable ends."

Countryman – rather my words be
pulped by the olive-press; by grape
treading-feet and thrashing elbow
than forget to breathe free
union of thought...

These opinions, drafted first as epigrams
deserve the roughest plywood case
to let the fearless elements in. Later, when
the last mask covers both our names there'll
come a constant whirring: no comforting

ends! Just nardoo, thistle, fleur-de-lis.

AFTER "A WINTER EVENING IN YALTA"

And... I am clothed in Brodsky's skin.
It is not alien. It fits
like a noble hand-me-down
with its old wearer still breathing
through voluble mendings.

The exile in me sees
a dissected day-break star lifting

        the dream-ship of Anna.
        The bloody Polish October.

New York City. Prague. The Great Divides;
there are many
cat-walks in your veins.
You house those cataleptics
yet they say very little these days.

Tell me, is it that
insomniac moon-lightings launch
only left-over salutations?
        "The Gods know if we'll
         see each other again..."

Friend Brodsky, I kiss the cataract
of your eye.
I hail the torn sky and
do my best to keep
our penetrative night-watch burning.

Clothed in your skin I too become
over-worn; twice as vulnerable.

ABOUT THE AUTHOR

Stefanie Bennett has published 13 volumes of poetry, 2 chap-books, a libretto & a novel. She has tutored in The Institute of Modern Languages at James Cook University & acted as a publishing editor. Of mixed heritage (Irish-Italian-Paugussett-Shawnee) she was born in Townsville, Queensland, Australia.